'We take pleasure in sending you this new book for review.

Title: *Space Traveler*

Poems by Benjamin S. Grossberg

ISBN 978-1-59732-118-1 (hardback)
ISBN 978-1-59732-119-8 (paperback)

$25 hardback • $14 paperback

Publication date: April 2014

Please send us a copy of your review. This will let us know you are interested in our books and assure that your name remains on the active Review List for future publications.

Many thanks.

The University of Tampa Press
401 West Kennedy Boulevard
Tampa, FL 33606
utpress@ut.edu
813-253-6266

Space Traveler

Space Traveler

Poems by

Benjamin S. Grossberg

UNIVERSITY OF TAMPA PRESS

Manufactured in the United States of America
Printed on acid-free paper ∞
First Edition

Cover painting by Autumn Von Plinksy
Engravings by Samuel Ringler
Copyright © 2014

The University of Tampa Press
401 West Kennedy Boulevard
Tampa, FL 33606

ISBN 978-159732-118-1 (hbk.)
ISBN 978-159732-119-8 (pbk.)

Browse & order online at
http://utpress.ut.edu

Library of Congress Cataloging-in-Publication Data

Grossberg, Benjamin S. (Benjamin Scott), 1971-
  [Poems. Selections]
  Space traveler : poems / by Benjamin S. Grossberg. -- First edition.
    pages ; cm
  ISBN 978-1-59732-118-1 (hbk : acid-free paper) -- ISBN 978-1-59732-119-8 (pbk : acid-free paper)
  I. Title.
  PS3607.R656A6 2014
  811'.6--dc23   2014008363

Contents

Home

In my mind's the planet: spinning,
iridescent as mother of pearl,
worn vitreous and smooth by waves
of space. Because of what I know
about the layout of the universe, I know
I am always moving toward it—
whatever direction I might travel;
it is parallel to every vector, a sharp
left at every star. And because of that,
although I can't find the planet
on any chart, have no coordinates
to plot (no X, Y, or Z axes),
I am confident I am getting closer.
It's like staring at a mirror as hard
as possible, in an attempt to see
yourself (beyond the deadened look
of a space traveler staring in a mirror),
as if you could see into the dilation
of your own pupils. In the blackness
of mine, I would see my planet:
iridescent ball floating in starless
darkness, and I'd touch down there,
kneel on an iridescent beach.
But then I remember I'm in a bathroom,
that there's nothing in the mirror
but the deadened face: moving
toward home (that must be so) so fast
it's strange to think I'm standing still.

Wandering

I didn't always wander. Once,
I had a small home with a garden.
A planet dweller lived there,
and we had the local equivalent
of a dog. It's hard to say
what happened, but at some point
I found myself converting parts
of our bungalow into a ship.
First appliances: fridge, stove,
electric tooth brush and water pick.
Then larger pieces. Siding
for the rocket body; chimney
for part of the nose cone.
Right now, I'm entering coordinates
into a combination of water heater
and wet bar. Both of us knew
things were finished when I
savaged the bed for springs.
(Landing apparatus.) Eventually
it was just the two of us
in a denuded frame, sitting
on the floor, not talking about
leaks, drafts. In the garden,
my ship flattened the winter squash.
It towered above what was left
of the roof. There wasn't much
of a goodbye. He shrugged and I
scanned the room for wire nuts.
(I forget now why I needed wire nuts.)
When my afterburn ignited
what was left of the place, I
allowed myself a small smile. Then
I set the toaster for deep
space. It didn't ding for years.

Wandering

Roadless vehicle: means that every
instance is a juncture, that every
path branches always—and in three
dimensions. This is the burden
of untethering wholly: all planets, all
places have equal claim, anywhere
become everywhere. I once put
roots down on a world in the most
literal sense: slid with my index finger
row after row of seeds into nearly
granulated soil: on all fours, palms
and knees roughening, darkening.
I crawled the field's length beneath
that planet's triple suns, saw at equal
spacing the nearly translucent cones
burst from the ground. And soon
how they uncoiled into spears.
There was no reason for the gladness
this occasioned in my heart, no cause
to adore the line after line of them,
that my hand seemed to raise them
higher and higher from the dirt, each
a marionette made to pull itself
up to full height. I think of them now,
looking out a window of this ship:
panning the scattering of stars,
themselves like seeds indexed into
the black loam of space. There was
a field that was my home, a world
I understood in the long silences
of its dawns. Now there's this:
stars thick and old as fire. In all
their history, none have cracked
open, no golden thread of roots
unwinding beneath them.

He Talks Frankly about Desire

Out here, the pull of bodies keeps
everything moving. Mass desires
mass, in even the tiniest quantities.
But what differentiates us, this
sentience, is that it isn't simply mass
that compels, but the idea of it:
the weighted notion, the notion
of waiting. A physics of our condition—
you might call it a strange force—
gives the dream of bodies more pull
than those orbiting close. It's as if,
human, your Earth suddenly tore
itself from the Sun, flung itself
chest first into the void, for the idea
of another: a sun whose conversions
were more compelling. You know
all gold's forged in a star's heart?
Well, it's as if your Earth lusted
for a sun that could generate better
luster. No matter the likelihood
of the planet spinning endlessly
forward—bowling ball (blue, marbled)
gliding on a never-ending lane toward
no pins. No matter that the star—
if it existed—might crisp it to coal.
The idea must be satisfied. But
I was going to talk frankly about
desire, wasn't I? Well, I desire
frankly: this dark is cold, and I
distinctly remember back there, still
pulsing, the place where I left my sun.

Tense

My species has one for nouns
in the process of passing: say,
a planet you no longer stand on
but which still exerts on you its
considerable tug, the fist
of its massy core reaching
up through groin and torso.
A way, then, to say, not *I am
on this world* or *I was*, but
that other state, the one
between. We use it to discuss
the dying—though usually not
to their faces—and dinner—
as plates are cleared—also love
in its last phases, the sharp
jerk before it, too, falls back
lifeless on the bed. Therefore
we listen especially carefully
to a soured beloved for
the inflection of ending:
that inflected ending (the slip
like a sheet of paper torn
lengthwise) added to a verb,
a susurrant gut punch.
Once, a planet dweller and I
shared years in this tense
reality as if his couch were set
on a cliff edge: moonless
planet in the sparsely starred
rim of the galaxy. We spoke
of ourselves, our common life
this way: never *we are, we were*—
but drawn out years
in a liminal mood. I started

to get used to it—and to him—
and imagined an entire
existence like that, hunched
under afghans in dark night,
feet over the edge, dangling.

His Husband

In terms of location, all I can say is
back there, and point to a patch
of sky: a place no thicker
or thinner in stars. In terms
of the quality of life, the color
and heat of its sun, atmospheric
feel on the skin, I can say
nothing. And yet nights—my ship
in the yard—I lay, a guest,
in one of their frame structures.
He was not the most acute
of their species; he failed to notice
that I needed a helmet to breathe or
that my limbs did not unfold (enfold)
like his own. Maybe he noticed
and didn't care. He brought bowls
of a limp green vegetable and we
ate beside each other in silence.
This was always in winter, always
with blankets he drew around us.
There was a moment before I left,
standing on the ship's retractable stairs,
back to the arched door: I saw him
watch me through the kitchen window.
It was night and the darkness of space
pressed right down against his lawn.
Well, it's years since that moment.
I have grown old in this ship, balled
like a worm in its silver pods.
And because I have been traveling
faster than light, nearly fifty
generations have slid between us.
(I am in fact the only living thing
that knows he existed.) But

it's also possible that I am caught
in that moment right now: still
seeing careworn eyes through a pane
of glass. A yellow incandescence
burns behind him, and both of us
wonder if I'm really going to leave.

The Doppler Effect

Because waves flatten as they
move past, the falsetto spiraling down
to a gravelly uttered base, I'm hard put
to say how anything sounds—
even the voices of those I know
most intimately as we move toward
or away from each other: approach
and departure distorting the notes
to birdsong or thunder. If two bodies
were momentarily perfectly still,
only then it seems could you have it:
the actual timbre. I imagine the two
of us on his floor, for a moment static—
not so much as aging at unequal rates—
and my body arced to receive
every decibel, the full wood grain
of his voice, so I could trace knots,
the looser and tighter lines, finger
years of drier and wetter weather.
I said *on his floor* but of course
we'd be on a bed: drifting
in the noiseless vacuum of space,
undistracted even by each other's eyes. . . .
On his planet, there's no patience
for such romantic claptrap; they
never bothered to outlaw sonnets
because the whole population simply
lost interest in them—but I think he
may be a closet heretic. I think he
still remembers the day I crash-
landed my ship in his drainage ditch,
and he came out with a pailful
of tools and never once appeared
to notice that I was an alien.

Later, on his dark patio, he took
hold of one of my wiry appendages
and told me that he loved me.
But I didn't catch the words. I didn't
need to. I was moved to perfect
stillness by his tone of voice.

Orbital Decay

I've been thinking about Earth's
orbital decay, wondering
if it's also in your thoughts—
like a slow leak in a balloon,
the incipient wrinkles that denote
change, like the evolution of a face
over decades, even a face you love.
How easy it is to ignore those wrinkles,
or, in half-light, to smooth them away
with your thumb, fingers cupping
the jaw line, the chin. Permanence
is not the province of planets:
evanescent things, their evolution
and revolutions, coalescing
with the birth of a star
then slowly spiraling toward it
with a controlled inevitability,
like a dancer twirling in
to her partner's arms. What can we
hope for, then, creatures who dig
ourselves up from the dirt
of shifting continents, themselves
lily pads on a strata of fire?
Surely we can't be blamed
for having our illusions, for
keeping them, willfully, as if
they were secrets from one another.
Sometimes, human, he calls me
and we speak as we did
when we saw each other often—
when we lived on the same world,
though that was in some unplaceable
back there of time and distance.
Around us, the universe swung

like a noon-hour clock shop:
bells and chimes, pendulums
and birds extending on wire, everything
moving, and here a German couple
emerged and dancing, revolving
on their spring together, telling time
rather than having it
tell them, as I suppose they could—
lucky couple—hewn, as they were,
on the same piece of wood.

The Great Moon Hoax, 1835

No hoax. They just didn't
hang around very long:
the blue unicorns, bipedal
beavers, the man bats especially,
which flew up in cork screws
and glided down with fully
outstretched wings. A hopping place
your moon, but that was back then—
existing, as all wonders do,
in the interstices created
by ignorance. Between question
and answer, blankness
and language—in that medium
of waiting—genius beads
on the skin: comes in such
excess that the body
drains it through all portals.
And this is why strangers
are so easy to love: because
blue unicorns bound
on their hills, because beavers
carry kindling bundles into
thatch huts, and if you squint
through the eye piece, you can see
curls of gray smoke come out
the chimneys. To mourn, then,
that I became to him
and he to me a thoroughly
known satellite? Not necessarily
granulated gray rock, but still—
the topographies all charted,
biological samples all already
lodged. Don't misunderstand me,
there was comfort, there

was safety, but nobody
travels a quarter-million miles
to revisit a derelict moon.

Notes

Ochre and blood glyphs—
first him spearing a boar, then
said boar spitted, flames
licking its bristled back. Ages
from now, human, only nutcases
on his world will realize the third
represents a rocket ship:
see, they'll say, *shape of nose
cone and fire shooting aft.* (His
rendition of my slow descent.)
One drawing more will be lost
to smoke rising from the boar's
charred flank: fishbowl helmet,
space suit, my mitted hands
in an open embrace—scientific
revolution scuttled by a desire
for boar well-done. But what
could they have made of that
interspecies love? So long ago,
human, I said goodbye
to the hot mouth of his cave,
felt Pleistocene ice ping off
my helmet as I crossed tundra
to where my ship gleamed like
nothing else on his citiless world.
So long ago, his cave soured
from primitive charm to
a frustrating naiveté, and I
whittled by the fire geometries
I knew his eyes weren't
trained to recognize. Meanwhile
he painted in ochre, in blood—
every morning a new image,
a note for me to wake to

while he was out on the hunt.
Ages from now his people will
reproduce those glyphs in art books,
admire the contour of rock
face and line. They will gladly
pay for such rustic grace.
Human, they are no fools.

His Dream

Love's what exists on yesterday's
planets: worlds defined by the lustrous
fires of exhaust and departure. Last
night I dreamed of a planet dweller
with encircling arms, maybe
half a dozen. I do not say I loved him,
but in the dream, he was the post
and I was tethered. I thought, held
back, but was with a taut snap
loosed, my hands reaching vainly
toward him, as if I were flying off
into a tornado towering above
the house. In the dream, there was
no house, except him, and I ran
inside, slammed the door, then
from room to room drawing shades.
When he held me the tornado
thinned and diminished until it
(with a bright pop) simply winked
out, and I breathed the long trek
toward morning. If two aliens
simultaneously dream of each other,
a wormhole opens, radiating tunnel
through space-time connecting
their ships like a string and two cans:
picture them huddled, children
in a midnight bedroom, the wilds
between forbidding and rare. *Can you
hear me?* Pause. *Yes I can hear you.*
And that's all—though a shroud
of sleep will soon descend again—no
other words. No other words needed.

His Nightmare

I'm at the control panel, leaning
my weight on the go lever,
pressing it hard into the console,
hearing squeak and drip
as the ship inches forward.
On a nearby planet: childhood
pet drowning. Ailing father
clutching his chest. Or
another space traveler ready
to jet off at light years per hour.
My ship squeaks, squirms;
the space traveler casually checks
hatches, pats the silver body
of his ship, a good Labrador. Then
a stairwell unfurls. I've got
something to tell him, something
urgent; it will make him remove
his traveler's mitts, extend
his hands to me. It must be said
now. I can see his back
as he mounts the stairs, which then
retract into the ship. Thrusters
fire. My ship's a pig cooling itself,
wallowing side to side. I lean
hard on the go lever. Harder—
then wake. Space is clear, moving
past at a good clip. The relief.
No other ship's ahead of me. No
other ship in the system or
cluster or it seems the whole
galaxy. No other ship at all.

His Husband

Is intermittent intercom, is planetlocked
at best, is dedicated—deeply dedicated—
to the soils he's always known, and loves
them. He loves also, it has been said,
the space traveler, a love he manifests
in a variety of subspace frequencies.
They talk about weather patterns:
what eyes circulate globeside
and out in the larger rotations of space.
What's it like out there this morning?
Absolute zero, airless. And by you?
Sometimes the space traveler wonders
how finally to differentiate love
from need, and if it's so bad that need
may be a needed scaffolding. *It's nice,*
I may go for a walk. Want to come?
Ha ha. Possibility: an old window
propped up by a dust pan. Though not
clairvoyant, the space traveler sees
their future. What he can't tell,
given the rotations of the galaxy,
is if the planet may be understood
as moving away from the ship, or if
the ship's to blame. But at any rate—
at an accelerating rate—their disjuncture
only increases, and the bursts of sound
increasingly lag. Soon, he knows
(maybe they both do), some message
will be their last—a plea, perhaps,
the answer to which will never arrive.

His Brother

Is not a space traveler. Lives
in fact on a planet the color
of parchment, but withholds
the address: those three little
coordinates (X, Y, and Z) that
a brother longs to hear.
Holidays the space traveler
looks twice at dust balls, at
rocks desiccated and pretty
much absolute zero. *Could
be down there*, he thinks,
bouncing a red ball against
its paddle. *Just the kind of
world he enjoys.* He sips soy-
milk from a juice box, muses,
*and what could a reunion
look like anyway?* Planet
speak, spacer lingo: even
a few decades of divergence
renders it impossible, with
common words denoting
skew experience: *travel,
food source, home, brother*—
the abyss after hello shrinks
the universe to a midsize
urban park. *There's always
next year*, he mumbles, easing
his feet into a tub of hot water.
Maybe I'll just stay up here.

His Father's Missing Brother

Picture this: on a planet at the edge
of a spiral arm, a kid brother leaves
an apartment. And never comes back.
As if the apartment door opened onto
the pull of space, and he fluttered out here,
arms and legs spread wide like Vitruvian Man—
like a kite diminishing against the sky
until the string snaps. Picture the phone
ringing in his apartment, the sparse
efficiency unkempt, a cereal box, banana
peel on the counter, work clothes in a pile
on the love seat, a button-down grayed
by urban heat. Decades follow, searches
flare up: newspaper ads; detectives
hired; internet scoured. But there's no way
to pull a body back from space, no finding
once it drifts beyond the first star, rips
the membrane between *here now*
and *then gone.* In the bluish light
of planet Heaven, father wakes
to his brother: twenty, as remembered,
in a scrolling, opalescent gown. Or
maybe he finds him in living faces,
the additive heaven of too much
aluminum accumulated in the brain.
It's hard to know how these things
get passed down, but clearly they do.
Sometimes I see him—tumbling
like a handful of jacks, revolving
Vitruvian Man—beyond my portal window.

The Great Filter

Somewhere, the choke—
what cuts off oxygen, makes
the internal combustion
of life sputter out. There's no
other answer to the paradox:
if life, human, then why
no evidence? Given the scale
of stars, the scale of years,
life ought to have left behind
a little litter, observable even
with your humble Hubble.
You wonder, don't you, if
you're there: that Panama
where continent thins to isthmus,
those shoals where species
break and dissolve in caps
of white fizz, as if there were
an inverse relationship between
intricacy and durability, and you
had just become a little too
complex for your own good.
I have, more than twice,
(for a few of your solar years)
mothballed this ship
in an alien's shed, have found
on his planet a cat-like creature
to leap from my dresser
to his, to curl on a shared bed—
have shut my eyes against
the seduction of stars. Then
it all winks out: devolves
into strangeness like an organism
dissociating cell by cell.
And soon I drift out back

with a rag and oil can, check
bolts and polish the ship's body
with a particularly loving hand.
If such a filter exists, human,
it doesn't help to know.
You will do what all species do,
what life does: fling yourself
against it again and again
until it breaks you, or you find
a way through.

Runaway Stars

O yes, barreling through the universe
as if shot from a giant cannon:
I picture them head down, charging
like angry ruminants, fiery horns blazing
in all directions. Of course the odds
are pretty good they'll miss any given spot
(say, my ship, your planet) but God help
the spot they don't miss: wouldn't even
register a bump, just scorch before
the shock of its approach scattered ash.
It's a kind of fury caused—apparently—
by a binary's disruption. One implodes,
the other explodes on some trajectory,
blazing an ashen road big enough
to park a dozen gas giants and still
leave room for a whole fleet of Hondas.
Everything in space travels: the notion
of stillness is just a placeholder,
an approximation that doesn't hold place
on most scales, over any length of time.
But it's also true that some things
travel more impressively than others.
A space traveler's dream? To hitch
a ride on one of those stars: to clutch
chaps-clad legs around its pulsing heat,
hold on with one hand while the other
reaches up toward coolness. How they
buck and flare in their disentangled fury,
how they charge off suddenly and terribly
alone. That's the dream: not to be
the one burned, the dolt in its path, but
to mount, to ride the swelling fire.

He Pities Humans

Tell me about you, in your
moment between secretive
oceans and practical space travel—
what navigable eternity you find
to correlate to inner darkness,
what lights to set against
the patterns of your pressed-
closed eyes. And the milky
darkness that shuts your world
from the stars: how do you know
what's inside without them?
How without a blank to reach
a fist into do you figure
what all's inside? Not that
the outlet's everything, mind
you, but how with all expressed
on such a small scale, to apprehend,
say, the grandeur of being lost?
I once knew a suburban den: dim
light, a brace of couches, books,
a melon-shaped device similar
to your telephone. The limit
of my universe was the fact
of gypsum. But now—even
on a bad day, when only dust
rushes past, when ether refuses
any other organization—I
have more than possibility. I
have myself: unfolding in
punctuated darkness, in all
that space between the stars.

His Contented Moments

Think of the way your thumb
held in front of you can cover
the moon. Granted, humans have
big thumbs and a small moon, but
there you are: in a corn field,
celestial bodies disappearing
behind your digits. At some distance
above the Earth (if you looked
down), your left foot would blot
North America. And farther up,
the planet become so small
you could stand on it only
as a ballerina, aloft on a toe.
A little farther, and you, human,
would become a space traveler.
So it is, sometimes, this ship
displaces the universe around it:
so far from all, the universe
recedes into a tangle—
a string of your Christmas lights
balled up in a box to stow
for next year. But lit.
And here's the odd part—
it does that even though
I'm inside it, a speck somewhere
amid brightness and writhing
wire. These moments
are unstable; they puncture;
are frail to corrosion by
elements that would extend
your periodic table into
a lord's banquet. But, human,
more than once I have wished
to take you up with me, to share

how what startles with immensity
can balance, cat's eye,
on the palp of one finger.

Sex

So strange how your bodies must
stay closed to survive, how you teem
at the walls of yourself: the pressure
your insides are under—
as if one could twist a cap and hear
the hiss of soul escaping.
But up here are species wondrously
permeable: who take into and release
from themselves with miracle ease,
in the way your hand, say, might
pass through a beam of light or how
you might dive into a body
of water. You've been wondering,
I know, about alien sex.
Though of course all sex is alien,
even within species, as if curiosity
were a biological dictate.
But the real stuff, what happens
up here among the stars—
the spasms and plasmas
of a thousand thousand unlikely
interfaces: how creatures of stone
spark like flint; creatures of liquid
combine into a single current
and then dissociate, branch off into
separate beds or simply freeze
into distinct layers, according
to their differing densities.
Look, human, only to your own—
none among you without (after
a fashion) desire, and none that, cast
in the soft filter of appetite, wouldn't
pique another's will. Well,
so it is with us: we need and find
and lose, and need and find.

Earth

I visited your planet. Rented
a small apartment and watched
a lot of *Star Trek*. Funny you
think space is "the final frontier."
Everyone up here knows
frontiers proliferate. Temperature
is my favorite. How deep
you can ride into fire, how its
color changes as it gets hotter.
All the heats no one's reached yet
are no less places to live, states
of matter (and mind) than
Freehold, where my rooms were.
Freehold's a nice town.
I hung up my space traveler's mitts
and walked Main, stopping
in Friedman's for salt sticks.
I saw it was a good life and
envied you, who never fantasize
about the frontier of fire. Except
I now think that you do, too,
even without having words
to describe it or a sense
of all the colors that fire
eventually turns. I realize
that probably makes it worse.

Boston

I once walked the streets with a native.
Beside me, he gesticulated, smiled,
pointed out bits of local color: here
a senator's house; there a high-rise
breezeway that led to the water front.
His hands conducted the city into place,
seemed to materialize the structures
he gestured toward. (I recognize
this is not a power humans possess.)
For a while, all was going so well.
My rocket ship hidden beneath
an overpass, my human suit fitting
snug, without the sort of bunchings
or gaps that would've given me away.
It seemed entirely likely he would
invite me to observe up close a few
more unusual aspects of human
interface. But then we stopped
in a store and I emerged with half
a watermelon, and proceeded to
unmask myself in a pink dripping mess.
So hard to stay contained in the filling
of desire: the fingernail scraping
of its green rind. *No, no, you're not
supposed to eat that part,* he said
slowly backing away, his palms
held out in front of his chest.
I looked up from the raw shell,
and it's then I fear my eyes began to
dilate differently: a split completely
wrong for one of your species.
O he still showed me what he had
to show, no less sloppy than myself
in the plying of his satisfactions.

But by morning, I had slunk back
to the overpass, to where my ship
lodged on its side amid wrappers,
rags, and old cardboard, its perfect
chrome now sullied by car exhaust.

Earth

There are thirteen thousand
manufactured objects—two inches
or greater—in orbit around
your planet right now. When
my ship pulls up, there are
thirteen thousand and one.
I enjoy being among so much
of your junk. It gets me closer
to the ethos of your planet—
ever expanding circles
of junk. At first I thought
it was disdain, but now
I see it's a way you have
of expressing ownership.
Circling, I scoff at TV and
what passes for "prepared food."
On my planet, no one uses
microwaves, and we all decided
the radio went far enough
in terms of in-home
electronic entertainment.
The space around us has
absolutely no orbiting junk,
only a few weather satellites
and a refueling station
with a small shop and liquid
hydrogen in three grades. Even
its bathroom floors are clean.

He Falls in Love with a Native

Over dinner. This time it happened
between soup and entrée, when
the waitress came back
to ask if he wanted more
oyster crackers. I told a joke,
and he insisted on guessing
the punch line for a full five minutes.
I watched his mouth spit out
possible puns, as if he were
in the blowing-bubbles phase
of learning to swim. He got
close. I went back to the salad bar
to clear my head, scooped up
too many chick peas and grew
afraid he'd comment.
People behind me were waiting.
Dare I put a few back? Over coffee
he asked for details about
this space-traveler life. I assembled
a rocket ship out of asparagus
using his leftover mashed potatoes
to mount them upright. There's
no point falling in love with humans.
Sometimes (in movies) one of you,
the displaced one—the one we
feel sorry for—the teenager
whose terrible foster parents get
eaten—that one will end up
boarding, will take the hand of some
bipedal outline in light. Truth's
shabbier. Old Toyota, radio playing—
he and I pull up to my rocket ship,
hidden in a stand of pines. I promise
vistas, possibility, a willingness

to continue the conversation even if
it takes all night. Your species
has perfected the shrug. *Then
maybe,* I say, *dinner next week?*
But I'll be a million miles away
by then. Probably.
If not, I'll plan my day around it.

He Addresses the Native, Sometime Later

At the moment I stopped,
what you didn't know was that
the ship also stopped: engines
cut; the radiant hearth, radiant
heart of its propulsion ceased.
It listed in sudden silence.
What you didn't know was that
comets stopped, gathered up
their icy tails like bridal veils;
and moons stopped: yes, in the
quadrant and beyond, hulking
and airless (those without air)
stopped and tides everywhere
reared up like fists to slam hard
on the checkerboard of dry land.
What you didn't know was that
planets stopped—around their
suns, a screeching halt that sent
landlubbing aliens flying
through windshields. And suns
stopped, for a moment their
fierce conversions stilled, while
inside, their hydrogen stores
cooled. Even the rotation
of the galaxy slowed, threatened
to stop, and might well have
done it had you not spoken.
What you didn't know was that
I was looking at your face, at
the contracted irises' china blue.
Your people have a saying,
the Earth moved, but they
have it (like so much else)
backwards—and of course
the scale's all wrong.

Crop Circles

It was me. An accident. But
like other mysteries begun
in accident, they achieved an
ex post facto purpose: a reminder
to your age which has forgotten
scale and the beauty of unexpected
vantage, like how a face looks
different beneath yours, how
proximity and angle either elicit
or create new expression. Fear,
for one. Or subtle notes
of pleasure—just a finger of it, two,
coming around a cracked-
open door. At the edge
of a crop circle, you may sense
a shape, a pattern, and even—if
you are of a metaphysical bent—
design: an inkling of arc,
a hint of more perfection
than available in an average
urban byway. This sense, this leap
of faith: until you can mount
the necessary height. Just so,
the contours of a face: eyes
like blue watercolor, for example,
a beard you'd call auburn—
well, I certainly had that much
faith and am constantly reminded
that patterns may be discernable
from variable heights: that what
currently looks like chaos
might—with the advantage

of better vantage—look a little
inevitable, a little purposed
by a hand in the stars.

Meryl Streep

But is it one thing, or many? Or perhaps
a kind of sapien banyan tree, some
root system connecting its various trunks?
Planet dweller, even among the stars, most
beings are freighted with only a single self—
obsessed, often oppressed by it, as
with time, as how to ease time's passage.
We are bowlegged (practically) river-
guides, or plutonium-rod fashioners
with feathered bangs. Never both.
We are stocky French chefs disarmingly
like other stocky French chefs, or frowzy
but secretly passionate Italian housewives.
One's enough. And yet: this singular
manifestation of Terran zoology—this
Streep. . . . Is it self-propagating, some
island rainforest its only native habitat?
If the whole could be transported (a crane,
say, for the heft of its ganglious rootball),
I'd gladly take it up with me, my sole
companion for this extended transience,
these lonely ages of aging between worlds.
How its tentacles would amuse—
octopus puppeteer—here, Miranda's
pointed glance at my shoes and her
tiny pursed mouth. Dare I giggle as she
dismisses me (*that's all*) from my own
Captain's Chair? There, Joanna's hug
as she surrenders maternal rights.
The pleasure as she and I both turn
blear-eyed back to the stars. (There'd be
increased twinkle.) I'd have to clear
whole decks, find an earthenware pot
the size of an Escalade, stock up

on water, whatever fertilizes it, and fuel
for the drag on the ship's engines.
But what I wouldn't give, planet dweller,
for such company—for so many selves
to beguile this single, burdenous one.

Home

Every globe warms, except
those that cool. Traveling
at the speed of light, I see
the evolution of planets
over millennia, local time:
mood rings for whole
populations. Yours shows
angering. I had one once—
a mood ring (also a planet)—
but it stayed blue because
my people have cold hands.
That means we have warm
hearts, except that we don't.
When Earth finally passes
fully to fretful violet,
I bet it will explode.
Happens to other planets,
why not yours? Could be
what happened to mine,
or it could still be out there,
turning color so I don't
recognize it. But my planet's
more likely to freeze, shatter
like a dropped chandelier—
for hundreds of years its dust
rising into the space around it.

The Oil Spill

It's all right. My species ruined
our planet, too. Chewed it, gouged it,
stewed it in any of a dozen flavors
of port, then ate it on toast. When all
was said and done, damn near
a billion of us stood back to back
on a tiny island, surrounded
by floating towers of plastic—
skyline of blues, greens, yellows, reds
bleaching in sunlight, and squadrons
of tern-like creatures circling above us,
squawks deafening. Certainly our
futures market seemed bleak.
And there you are with a hole
in your mantle, puncture wound
caused when you were about to
carve the turkey and someone
knocked into you (though it sure
looked like suicide). Mercutio-like
final gesture: your ironic observation
that at least now you wouldn't
have to scrub the roasting pan.
You do your best to halt the black
hemorrhage, pinching your side
between thumb and forefinger.
Good luck. If planets had viscera,
yours would be splashing out
with the rupture, uncoiling
on the surface like so many miles
of crude-soaked boom. But you're not
the first: think of my species, scads
and hordes, all our mouths forming
Os of disbelief, all of us noticing
in the plastic bergs the wrappings

of our favorite brand of breakfast bar.
Maybe it's in the nature of change
not to come until it's too late—
but then it does come, and we shut
our mouths, and someone starts to
scare off a few of the terns by
screaming and waving his arms.

His Calculus

You? Your fate was sealed the moment
you set a ring of stones around a fire:
in some Neanderthal night, the collective
tremor of northern species, and global
air circulation pausing a moment
to apprehend change. I'd like to think
the stars, too, clarified in translucent
darkness, that for a moment all
burned blue, looked down
in an earnest convocation.
What to say, human? That generally
by the time a trajectory becomes clear,
it's essentially completed? That causes
swim in conclusions? Now you know.
Now I know, too. And though
from up here I'm unable to help you,
I will say—pondering your world—
no destination seems so important, no
work trumps my attention like your
gloved hands, tenderness conducted
through latex and scrub brush toward
all those small lives you have ruined.
Perhaps a few decades from now,
an interstellar cavalry will arrive—
do-gooder species watching your
accelerating bleed, moved, will pull
you back from the ledge by the X
of your crossed suspenders, will deposit
you and such Earthly life as remains
on a pristine world. Imagine
the pods launching out like bees
from a flaming hive, the furious drones
cooling with distance, and then
the landing—chrome studs among

long grasses, a field wide as Kansas.
Fanciful? Had I been there, human,
I'd have poked the Neanderthal
on the shoulder, tapped my snappish
foot until he handed me that first rock.
Then I'd have clocked him with it.

Restless Leg Syndrome

I'm not laughing at you. Really.
If one takes the long view, as
being so far out in space
I must, it's clearly just the first
step in your race to cure
restlessness. It may be that large
parts of the galaxy peer anxious
at your adventures in pharmaceutica:
your population-wide control groups,
your willingness to start nearly
in utero. (It is your dedication
that astounds us.) We have
no doubt you will still the throbbing
leg, the palsied hand, will in fact
find eventually an L-Dopa for
the restless heart. Worlds
in the system of galactic
commerce you may soon
become part of, each have wares
to give and take. You will take
a lot of getting used to, but
clearly pills will be your entry
into this intra-star bazaar. Among
the tight roads of a Kuiper Belt,
your representatives will hawk
from behind tables filled with row
after row of amber bottles. And,
human, I'll be there—will even
have helmet in hand as I ask
what blooms in your chemical
orchards, those gardens of mortar
and pestle. The day you sing out
restless leg; restless hand; restless
heart, I'll find an appropriate

copper penny, will cover the entire
cavity of my mouth with my palm
as I throw a double dose down.

Depilation

Because I have something very
much like ears, I have something
very much like tweezers. Vanity
a function of consciousness? Ask
all those elephants looking in mirrors,
trying to rub chalk Xs off
their foreheads with their trunks. But
"vanity" is too harsh: a preferred
image of self, merely—whatever
tentacles or spines, arms or buck
teeth, freckles or oleaginous
antennae. It's a grand thing
to be a space traveler, to observe
up close the multitudinous terrors
that pass in this or that galactic
neighborhood for beautiful. And
to learn also the ways in which
they sort of are. Travelers of all
kinds in ships only recognizable
as such by their ability to move. Each
new encounter expands the word,
adds new adjectives to the lexicon
of desire. Beautiful: some species
braid the most unsightly of hairs,
others take depilation to a
frightening extreme, making the best
of their organs look like underwater
fruit. So what? All are beautiful.
And all, once had, exist only
to be lost. But even in your limited
spectrum, you know that, don't you—
you with your hairy ears and eerie
hairs, and all those technological
advances you've made

on the tweezers; you who are so
utterly unlike me, and yet
whom I've learned to find beautiful.

He Pities Humans

Roy G. Biv is a friend, but only
one of many. Sound, too, in ranges
that jerk your dogs' heads sharply around,
a hard calligraphy on air to spring
the radar dishes of their ears. Listen
in whatever range you can, human—
it's not that you know dust only
in handfuls, but that the tools
by which you know it make it
only dust. Out here are creatures
who see in it the handiwork of God:
not in the cheesy metaphorical manner
of your evangelicals, but with beautiful
literalness, the fine-handling fingerprints
of the first cause smudging the glass
of each grain. So I don't blame you
if hearing silence where is music
beyond your range you nominate
nothing, or if you end after violet
the spectrum of visible light. But
even on your world, the least of you
discharges colors he can't see, his body
dispelling silence in nearly all registers.
Imagine yourselves as I see you—
even the reduced form looking back
from a bathroom mirror, woken
too early, when outside's a snowy
morning he has shortly to enter.
It is an odd irony—a ready excuse
for all your cynicism, even the chewed
aluminum of your politicians—that
you of all creatures are denied sense
of your own radiance.

The Planetary Observer

Pretty soon, your people will give up
the concept of time, that quantity
you discuss as if it had fixed meaning:
like a bedeviled middleschooler
trying to solve for one variable
too many, his teacher snickering
behind a grade book. Time is,
finally, quantifiable only on an
individual basis: each of us
in his own bubble, an experiential
oxygen tent. Do you know
what it is like, planet dweller?
Like a ship in this airless void.
Between your bubble of time and that
of your intimates: infinity, perpetual
present, or nothing at all—just
the cold energy of empty space.
You think in your bedrooms
it collapses; you think practicing
the ways bodies plug into bodies
might connect you, if briefly, into
a single appliance for tracking time.
Or you think words can do it, incant
you into, transport you toward—
not a magical other place (how
easy, how common) but into an elusive
shared time. This explains, maybe,
what you feel afterward: the heart-
rending separation, the time bubbles
bouncing each other back like an
endlessly supple rubber. (Always
separated by rubber.) What can I say,
human? I do understand. Maybe
I was too quick to judge you.

His Hope

You think days between worlds?
Think years. And me
in my Captain's Chair: a statue
festooned with cobwebs, a small
spider hanging off my face.
Then something beeps.
I flicker to life. Chips of plaster
crack off the first joints I rustle:
what you might call fingers,
the fluttering of what functions
like eyelids. The viewscreen
crackles, flashes, the start of a film,
and a world fills my vision—
the blooming saturation
of its atmosphere (plastic wrapper
on hard candy) under which
anything might have evolved.
Even a race of travelers who've
learned the lure of stop signs,
who've come to prefer billboards
to movies, sofas to bicycles, who'll
take me in as a wayward brother.
I imagine them in silver robes,
a convocation circling my just-
landed craft, sad and sagacious
as I descend the gangplank,
my pockets full of beads and
cigarette lighters. Their chrome
collars turn up like noir raincoats;
they lead me to their village—
a few dozen chrome mushrooms
bursting from a gray escarpment.
And this is the part of the story
where I'm never heard from again,

not even years later when you
send down a party to look for me.
But I was there. I was the one
with the plate in his lip, only
the plate was chrome and my species
doesn't have lips. That platform
you stood on with your bullhorn,
shouting my name into the crowd?
That was the ship. Or part of it.
The rest became the casing for a well.

The Promised Planet

The practical infinity of space
has long been a great comfort.
Your ten thousand monkeys
clacking ten thousand years
exist already on ten thousand
planets, churning permutations
of every document you've
ever written: a comma cut
or added, burdensome semi-
colon or imprecise conjunction.
In effect, then, all destinations
lie in all directions, and speed
displaces trajectory as the
resonant variable. Important
question is, are you moving
fast enough to get there before
something—death—stops you?
(It is like navigating in an
apple tree: the same world hung
glistening red everywhere.
You have only to reach your
hand out far enough to take
the world you are after,
palm it from off its star.)

His Viewscreen

Sometimes I just sit and watch it.
At any moment: something
might click. Or beep. Or ding.
Things come forward, float
up from the ink of space
like the message in a magic 8-ball:
a planet that says *Yes* or *No*
or, more likely, *Ask again later.*
I'm amazed how this activity
consumes hours, each a fish
lowered into its gullet by the tail,
pulled out as picked-clean bones.
I check instruments, scan
stars; as the scans load, I check
other instruments and scrutinize
other stars: I enlarge them
then shrink them again, letting
each traipse across the stage
of my attention. Like conflict,
crisis, and resolution, there's
a narrative arc: anticipation,
scrutiny, and disappointment,
which switches quickly
back to anticipation as another
star loads. The fantasy's clear—
that one will shine with
the fullest possible light, will
invite me up on stage with it
or pull something of me
through the viewscreen
out into space. The word
may well be "correspondence."
On these nights, I go to bed
in a particularly exhausted

non-exhaustion: although I find
myself tired, I have not moved,
in any sense, for hours.

His Aisling

The man came to me as a planet,
veered from the void with wind-combed
grassland under a skull cap of polar ice:
imposing on my viewscreen as if space
had suddenly rendered its center,
which of course it had (another
center). The compelling gravity
of its iron core seemed to tell me
that wherever I thought home was,
home was here. So I gave my ship
to its surface: took it down
to the body revolving beneath me
until body touched body. In time,
the engine burn cooled. Or was it
that the planet came to me as a man?
And I thought I could live on him—
stranger who stepped from his ship
as from a desert: the dark leather
of his boots, of his skin lightened
by dust powdering each hard step.
I dreamed of a new ship then, of
side-by-side Captain's Chairs; thought
how on the common armrest our
elbows might touch, how he might
not withdraw his. In my vision,
his dust slaked the thirst it created
and I lived as if in a native element—
the landscape of his face, a flashback
from a moment in childhood
I had long since forgotten.

His Crush

Interestingly, it puns the same
in my language, too. Think
soda cans, think trash compactor,
think an enormous industrial
apparatus that squeezes and stacks
old cars. And how all these shrivel
beside the compaction of a heart
in the twin grinding knuckles
of desire. He wants to tell me
it doesn't work that way, not
at my age—though he and I
reckon years by different suns,
so he has no idea how old I am,
not really. I want to tell him
I am as old as the wisdom
he hopes for in a lover, as young
as the incarnation of desire:
which must be beyond age, as
beyond gender, beyond species—
a lithe blue flame that manages
to warm even those parts of the body
decades cold. Listen, I tell him,
speaking into the intercom,
my voice moving out beyond
the ship—vector as the crow flies—
I don't want to compromise
our friendship, but I'm willing to try
if you are. Except I don't tell him,
and it's the air vent I'm speaking into,
not the intercom, getting dust bunnies
in my face. Soon we will meet
to hike an asteroid. Then
I will swing by his planet to watch
a flick on his world's crude

Internet. We'll sit on his couch,
as we do, and he'll lean his head
to the side—over a little further, then
a little further, until it seems almost
inevitable that it would float
to a soft landing on my shoulder,
like how you can cut the engines
and let your ship drift those last
few feet to touchdown.

He Warns Another Traveler

Think of Daphne, chased by the dirt-
crusted hands, calling out to the darkness
of space, which saved her in a chrome
transformation: her skin glittering
to silver, and where the balls of her feet
struck up dust, now fires and building
exhaust. Think also of our hike
on that craggy planet, how few words
we spoke of each other's tongue.
Each word a ledge, an outcropping
over rocky spires. I imagined us both
spitted. But I knew, and the knowledge
formed an armature for kindness,
that you were like me—knew it from
what I think were your eyes (hard to tell
behind the fogged-up helmet) and how
you knelt toward the soil to point out
the gnawed stumps of trees: something's
teeth, you said, had eaten them toward
an hour glass; it had backed off without
shouting timber. Under my space mitts,
my hands itched to feel yours. Our laughter
created brief islands of coolness
as if the foliage had thickened or one
of the suns had ducked behind a cloud.
Then we arrived back at our ships,
which hadn't incorporated, mechanical
fins not reaching out, wires not braiding.
The shielding did not open like robes,
like two creatures enfolding each other
in their rain coats. Think, brother
traveler, as you speed away from me,
of Daphne—thrusting upward through
the closing circle of the god's arms,

the smoke trail showing her ascent
and the fires that must have seemed bright
even against blue sky and sunlight.
Think of her alone on an endless path
through the galaxy, of her traveling
and traveling and traveling.

He Inquires of a Visitor

Treadmill facing a rear window,
I run full speed at the starscape
I leave behind: sweating
toward the past as I'm dragged
into the present. So hard
finally to decide if consciousness
is a forward motion. But it is—
I know it is—landing on new planets
and beating back (chair, whip)
those lions of perception that
threaten to chew them to the pulp
of *is like.* As seeing you
here in the present, which
your presence makes feel
like the past, I struggle to pry
the moment free of its history—
crowbar, hammer, one foot
up for leverage—and have
little luck. How did you get here,
watching DVDs of 90s Earth sitcoms,
eating a doughnut and leaving
an intolerable brush of crumbs
in my Captain's Chair? Do you
realize your dog is shedding
on my microfiber throw? Half-
convinced you are a figment,
I reach out a hand to pass it
through your form, perhaps
disperse you in a swirl of blue
mist. Last night I had a dream
of waking from a dream. In it,
you were already awake, returning
from the bathroom: only light
on in the ship, and I saw

your silhouette approach, bending
toward me in concern. *What?*
you asked. *Is it some kind of*
nightmare? What are you saying?
Then my palm comes to rest
dead square on your chest.

He Addresses a Correspondent

So many missives. And each an attempt
to say and not say, as if direct
statement had undone itself—
a candle melted flat into the table.
Do they reach you? Do you stroll
out to your mailbox to find the red
flag lowered, envelop hanging out
like a crab's fighting claw?
The stamp is from no Earthly polity.
You soak it off in water; take out
a magnifying glass to study
the alien flower, its stigma an eye
that winks at you. Do you read
the script? On warm nights, you ride
your V-Max under the stars. I fly
my ship over eastern Ohio; make
a semaphore of the fins; toot
the engine fires in Morse Code.
Others take out cell phones, post
videos on the Internet. But the text
was for you: who keep your vision
level, your legs spread as wide
as if you were mounting a horse.
You know, when you ride
you look like the Marlboro Man:
it's the set of your jaw, the cool
hardness, as if your skin were a metal
just lifted from snow. You remove
your helmet; sparse blonde hairs
explode upward. I suddenly become
shy and zoom off behind the tree line.
Did you see me? Sometimes I think
you keep your understanding
to a studied minimum, limit the size

of its cage and what you feed it,
knowing how—if it got too large—
it might take over the house. Start
demanding walks. Want your bed.
You'd have to reckon with it then.
You'd have to follow it through to
troubling conclusions. Other times
I sit balanced on my ship's nose cone
like a spinning plate and pluck
flower petals, letting each float off
into space. Imagine them settling on
the surface of your world's atmosphere—
drifting down to the vitreous blue
of a mountain lake. He loves me?
I think not. If they fell far enough,
every petal would burn.

His Duende

Sometimes I pull the ship right up
to the redline of a black hole, firing
the engines at ninety-percent thrust
just to hold steady. Around me
lesser ships shriek, throw their arms
in the air, and get sucked backwards—
into the vortex, a black annihilation.
Their captains can be seen panicky
and weeping through their viewscreens.
I sip tea, pinky out, and leaf
through catalogues. Dust streams in
from all over the galaxy, accelerating
past in glistening rills. I know
the stakes are real when I feel myself
lurch backwards. I drop the cup, which
cracks with a single clink. A sidelong
nervous smile, then I hurl myself
over the console, all my weight falling
on the go lever. Now the engines kick
into high whine, and my irises get
so tight the pupils threaten to sweat
out of my face, each a drop of black ink.
I start jettisoning things: appliances, old
furniture I'd hoped to refinish. Once,
a small wing of the ship: pressed
a few buttons and corridors detached,
fell back into the void. Then the ship
starts to crawl forward, and then a little
faster, and then faster. Soon, I am out.
Sometimes the black hole is another
space traveler. Usually, it's just
the memory of one.

Why He Declines

Because the body is both a ship
and the universe that ship explores.
Because all ports of destination
are ports within the body. Because
whatever wisp the self is can move
in the grand expanse from hand
to elbow, can tingle up to shoulder
and into viscera. The planets
of lung and liver, the gas giant
of stomach, the iron-cored heart:
because the self on each of these worlds
is a space-suited astronaut kicking up
gray gravel, planting a flag of discovery.
Offers come—casual and engraved—
as if the self alone can't navigate
whatever pathways exist in the body,
can't trip wormholes of imagination
to locate any exact flavor. Exact
savor. It isn't that interior is a perfect
microcosm of exterior, but that
when all's concluded the mesh
of memory just isn't fine enough
to sift the difference. So why, when
somewhere in the broad chamber
of the self, the invitation's answered—
a zone of desire, a series of sensations
between the coordinates of mouth,
groin, and stomach: and in the tiny
ship, a tinier ship (closing the eyes
can aid in navigation), I touch
down there, marvel at colors
in the methane clouds. *It isn't,* I
politely explain, *that I don't
want you; just that I don't need you.*

Black Holes

To just once say yes.
So many phenomena, so much
beauty that can be seen from
no safe vantage. Others
return from these regions—
desire's event horizon, passed
the shimmering rim, say,
of a black hole. *Accelerate,*
they tell me, *toward it: let*
your vessel enter it, and it
will enter you; give yourself
to a new experience of time.
They tell me that my failure
to understand is manifest in the
fretting lock moments have
on my consciousness: but I will,
I would, taken deep in along
with time, to where time's held
fast—a rope wrapped once, twice
around a fist, then allowed
to slacken. *A new sense of time,*
they assure me, *is a new sense*
of self. Metaphysical
hogwash of course, but I can see
they know something I don't;
can see their bodies know it,
and realize that as we have bodies
it is good for them to know things.
Still, I take my ship only
to the verge: corona of suction,
the place from where it can just
resist. And see theirs fly fast,
plunge into a realm of ink: running
lights drawn in ahead of them.

In my Captain's Chair, I hang
my head, a hand clutching each
control: the one that would
jolt me forward—then cease
to matter—and the other, hard
by my right, the knuckle-
white emergency brake.

Why He Accepts

When two arcs seem likely
to intersect, it's not inconvenient
to halt in space, to let the silence
of halting become another
sort of territory to fly through
for a while. This medium
is filled with anticipation—
because it's never clear
what form life will take or
if that traveler will appear at all.
It's also filled with wondering
at the wonder: why the shaking
hands, the pacing corridors,
why the shallower breaths?
Movement through this
territory is ragged. Then
the beep comes, the alert
that another ship approaches—
and silence opens up to jangle,
a rush of it as ships prepare
to interlace their clinking skins,
to fashion a bridge in the vacuum
where creatures nothing alike
(except in essentials) can
cross, can for a spell mingle.
The jarring lock, the suction
of vacuum withdrawing,
the lifting of eyes and intake
of breath toward another face:
no wonder the tremor. It even
sounds like too much. Though
most of the time the beep
never comes, and anxiety
subsides toward the usual

movement: the outward one,
the one that mesmerizes
with streaks of white light.

Black Holes

From inside, stars and everything
appear to rush away, getting
smaller and dimmer as you stare,
but snapping back to right size
when you break the gaze.
I meet other travelers there
in other traveler ships. After
we have established no
hostile intent, sometimes I
visit them through a thin
umbilicus, clear plastic tube
rustling in the current. My hands
guide me forward on a single wire,
and I can see ships parked
all around, defying dimension
like an Escher print. Then
the hatch opens, an alien
reaches a hand, and I float
through the vessel's confines.
An hour or two passes
before the hatch cracks again:
space traveler's silhouette (with
fishbowl head) appears, starts
back in the other direction.
It's me; visit's done. I fire up
the engines and break
the hole's gravity. No matter
what species they are,
they are so much like me
I mope for days. I stare
longingly out the portal
or slump myself over
a console, inconsolable.

His Pirate

Black, black, black. Moving
through space is moving through
time, as I measure distance in light
years, light days, light hours,
and measure time in distance:
fifty light years from a conversation
in which my name became a shriek,
and farther still from other voices—
the dock of ship upon ship,
portal opening to portal allowing
a soul to peer through as easily
as hand over hand up a ladder.
Some thousand light years ago,
I met a pirate whom I no longer miss
though I miss my awe of him: black
galleon in black space, no running
lights. His ship could silently rise
from underneath and clamp
onto the body of another ship
like a hungry spider. He recognized
in me a fellow, so we traded wares
as space travelers sometimes do, then
he fell away. Black into blackness.
There's no returning to the moment
when the portal closed, octagonal
of light diminishing and diminishing:
manhole, dinner plate, fist, eye—
finally a period ending the entry
about us in the journal in which
I recorded that meeting, dated
by vectors and the nearness of stars.

His Moon

Tucked behind an obscure gas giant,
tiny, shaped like a kidney bean—
but I had it registered as mine
for a small fee and now have
a certificate to hang in the ship
and a place to visit on holidays
and for picnics. The sky's dominated
by a ringless planet rarified enough
to float in a bathtub (a large one)—
and planetrise is watching
the curtain lift at a grand opera:
orchestral swell; swirls and storms
near enough to touch, as if a finger
dipped in its surface might ripple out
progressively larger circles. Certainly
there's no air or vegetation and very
little gravity. No place is perfect.
I dream (what kind of space traveler
wouldn't?) of planting organic
ground cover, having contractors
put in an atmosphere and a nice
surface liquid. Perhaps one day,
a species. At some point, the notion
of making overtakes the notion
of finding. Because there was
a planet inhabited by creatures
like me, where I saw silhouettes
in the rockface and even weeds
had a pleasant familiarity, doesn't
mean there is.

The Promised Planet

All right, no one promised. And yet
my very medium seemed to tingle
with the likelihood, as if suffused
with silver filings that captured the light.
Or maybe the odds just felt with me—
so many worlds, so many strains
of evolution, surely no biosphere
predicted the shape of any other.
One it seemed would have to meet
even those desires I hadn't yet
formulated, the latent tastes, needs
about to bloom in petals much larger,
more saturated than I had expected—
a vine unknown to itself, its own
tendrils and traveling, how its stamen
would center, the shape of its flower.
I once observed such a vine
up close, the hollow green flutes—
saw that it produced blanched nubs,
blunt fingers poking toward
the soil of its world. I wondered
how it knew, how it decided when
and where to put forth those nubs, if
it could sense in the undersoil some
needed liquid or element. And if so,
perhaps I, too, could do that: could be
my own divining rod—bare forked
stick that trembled at discovery.
You understand, it felt possible
then. So world after world passed
underneath me. Each time,
I checked myself for trembling.

Meaning

Human, when I think of "meaning"
as a planet, I imagine its perfect
lushness: rainforest-dense with pure
steam rising from its moist soils
and even its insects as beautiful
as jewels, beetles you don't
want to brush off your skin
because, whatever their iridescent
creepiness, they still signify
in convincing ways. But then
I realize the planet's just as likely
to be a desert: waves of sand,
parched air that cracks mucus
membranes into dry riverbeds—
painful crevices deep into the body
so the grit of meaning can lodge
right up in there. The anonymous
remains of other travelers
protrude from the dunes
(in the windstorms of meaning, even
the most ingrained identities falter),
but I trudge forward, space suit
draped with black cloth. I slant
into the storm toward an oasis—
I'm sure I see one—which is not
meaning but may well be
some accommodation with it.
In the distance, space travelers
lounge on deck chairs and sip
fruity drinks through long straws.
They're not even sweating.
They either know more than I do
or have found more pleasant ways

to know the same things.
But then I realize it's also possible
they look at me through their own
gritted-up fishbowls, imagining
a little Acapulco where cabana
boys fan me, bring me ice
shavings sticky with peach juice.

Time, Alone

Spend enough time alone
and the difference muddies:
external, internal. Walking
the corridors of the ship,
walking through ideas—
chambers merely platforms
for lingering: a memory,
a possibility, choices
revised or pending. As if one
were one's own homunculus
and the ship a larger self, though
that suggests a nearly infinite
regression of selves, a series
of Russian dolls with the merest
grain in the center: identity
reduced to an essential fact—
dust mote in an otherwise
sterile room. That's as good
a figure as any for this ship
wandering the vacuum
of space, the way the ship
catches starlight, glistens
as it falls toward or away
from absolutely nothing
like itself. In the cockpit,
I linger with the idea of time,
chagrined that the process
does not slow it, and where
I sleep, inhabit the notion
of alone, suspect it would be
little different in company.
At best, I find peace in how
these vectors answer each other:
ashes to ashes, dust to dust.

Life Expectancy

Because our experience of time accelerates—
as each single day becomes progressively less
relative to our lived experience—a week
would eventually feel like a second, a month
like a minute, and a year a mere turn
about the room. Therefore to live forever
would be to have one's final, dying moment
drawn out eternally. So I sit chagrinned
in my Captain's Chair, knowing the journey
from star to star will never take longer
than it does right now, and mourn my lost
boredom, which is also lost youth. If
there's compensation, it's that (I've heard
it said by the wise creatures, by those
who sleeping in space can be mistaken
for planets, as they dream eons around
blue stars) at the moment of death
the perception of time slows to near ice:
a dust mote can take millennia to fall across
a sunlit window, time enough (as you
watch from your hospital bed) for a race
to evolve on it, a civilization to rear
on its cratered surface, glinting in sun—
time for its denizens to grow, war, mature,
to evolve a literature, for you to get distracted
from a simple question, by the words of their
greatest playwright as his heath-bound king
surrenders to madness. Maybe your answer
is *yes* or *no*, or *I'm ready now*, the sound
of which never quite makes it up
from your chest, never passes your lips.

Time Travel

To creatures who exist beyond
the fourth dimension, we appear
as snakes, long segmented
bodies writhing through time.
At one end, the babies
we once were (rattles);
at the other, the decrepit men
we'll become (fangs). Time
never oppressed me before
I launched into space. Now
I pine for differentiation. Even
stars can tick by like sagebrush,
red mesas, the occasional cop
parked behind a cactus.
Revisiting the past ties you
in knots: was I in a desert once?
A desert planet? With another
space traveler in the side car?
I can't remember if time
made a third. I once asked
a creature of the sixth dimension
if, when 3D beings like us
share our lives, we seem
to intertwine like a caduceus.
He slapped his knee and said
that was a good one.

His Funk

Once, the ship broke. I was
nowhere (almost literally) and
functions failed: left and right.
Started small. I lost
the cigarette lighter: red ring
conveniently located by
the Captain's Chair. Shrugged.
Then speakers went. Then
refrigeration and heated seats—
finally lights all over the ship
winked out and even the go lever
wouldn't go. It got so bad, I
didn't want to try anything, just
assumed functionality. (Better
not to know.) There I was,
tense in my Captain's Chair
in the dark, drifting sideways
in a star desert: tiny, unnoticeable
thing waiting I suppose to cycle
through what fresh atmosphere
remained, to choke on my
own exhalant. I'm not sure
how long I sat like that before
with an awful jolt everything
kicked back on, like a power
outage fixed after midnight—
fridge, television, lights, stereo
blaring all over the house.
No sense of continuity, just me
rising from where I'd slumped
hours ago, wondering at
the world in which I'd come to—
how garish it seemed, how far
outside time, how suddenly
fragile.

Google Universe

From the farthest remove, the scalp swirl
of a head. Maybe. (From where
is the vantage?) You click in and each hair
diffuses into an arc of galaxies: blonde
twists of light. And soon the arcs
separate, grow away from each other as if
each were alive, each strand thickening
into increasing space. (How is it that light
can be composed largely of darkness?
Where are the satellites taking these images?)
Closer in, the galaxies themselves
diffuse. From the tight white clumps—
balled worms—one suddenly centers,
grows softball-large on the screen, then
it, too, opens to reveal dark spaces
(how is it that light . . .) especially out
toward the arms, each starting now
to separate from the sides, one pulling up,
the other down. Soon the galaxy fills
the viewscreen, which now zooms forward
toward pinpricks of light, individual stars.
But for this to be fun, we've got to click
closer in, still closer—until—there,
right there—in a particular field of space:
one of the pinpricks elongates to nose
cone, engines. It's the ship! And—
re-center, just a few more clicks now—
there's me! Aerial view. Swirl pattern
of my head staring at the viewscreen: me
staring at me staring at me staring at me,
afraid to look over my shoulder for fear
I might discover I'm not the original one.
Still, it's gratifying (or maybe I mean,
it's a relief) to have finally found myself—

even if the image is a little grainy, even if
there's a slight delay as I beam in from
wherever it is those satellites are.

Wisdom

All the gift of the listener:
the alchemy's in the ear alone.
(Or whatever organ's receiving
sense; on your planet, I believe
that's called an ear.) Sometimes
I meet another space traveler
who likes how I listen and calls
my occasional limp promptings
wisdom. I glow and preen
in adulatory light: but always
aware the honor's unearned.
Think of dust specks in a ship's
filtered breathable medium—
with what painful rarity
they smack into bulkheads, and
the ring of it, the waves
of sound rippling out from
impact. How taut, fine—
a silk smoother than silk—
the ear drum, how intricate
the cochlear spiral, to hear
such a sound, to identify
its cause and key. Think of
a space traveler's head
jerking toward it. In the bleak
blacks of space, sometimes
we learn to hear that sound,
learn to be grateful for it, learn
in our silent isolations even
to call it wisdom.

The Book of Wisdom

Contains no end of falsehood.
It says, *only unmet desire
can keep you from aging.* Says,
*only other beings can anchor you
to time.* It shows pictures
with saturated velvet colors:
stars exploding, stars being born.
Swears, *you'll grow casual
about sights like these.* And,
*other wonders will be yours
alone.* I quote: *the universe,
large enough for each of us
to happen on singularities
daily.* A copy is nestled
somewhere inside each ship:
under the Captain's Chair, stuffed
inside a hatch or bulkhead.
Like motel Bibles, they're
consulted by the desperate
no more than by the bored:
leafing through pages while
in the bathroom, a stranger
runs water and takes too long.
When the door opens, half
the mystery will fall away.
The Book of Wisdom has
a passage applicable then, too:
the next planet is always better,
it promises, *bluer, redder,
and nearer than you think.*

Heaven

Is yesterday, which is why
all stories of a Fall involve a new
sense of time. But the heavens
are up or out, which is why
travel pushes them farther back:
beyond oceans, planet, stars.
Both are mythically peopled—
gods, angels, idealized versions
of ourselves, fantastical aliens
(say, one head, two eyes, three
colors on their traffic lights)—
and both promise to answer nearly
unposable questions: what happens
when you die, or travel faster
than something really fast? Also
both lay claim to certain mysteries—
how the universe began and how
(when) it will end. The generous
among us imagine that travel
along a third vector—inward,
inside—might answer these
questions, too, but there aren't yet
rocket ships to go there.

Heaven

Don't say Heaven; say the heavens.
Say the movement through time
in this body and the movement
through space in this ship
collapse at the moment of passing
some particularly spectacular
Devil's Tower or Crab: the scattering
of hot oxygen in all its brilliance.
And beyond, say a veil lifts
in this darkness, the sheerest
scrim of perception without which
the stars, though still the stars,
are clearer in their yellows,
reds, and blues that are still
the same yellows, reds, and blues.
And let there be still the jewel
of the occasional solid planet, and
still let the ships of other travelers
cross my path like the random
radiation of a new idea. In short,
tell me the change will be all in me
and that I'll be there to admire it.

God

I hear there's an Earth species
("bear") that can give birth
while hibernating in a cave
little bigger than its body.
I imagine the cub crawling
blind and wet from the folds
of its mother, groping
helplessly for warmth in the
unaware flesh. According
to some, that's just how God
initiated the universe: galaxies
tumbling out one by one, rolling
like pinwheels in an attempt
to wedge in close, and God
on his side, hands pressed
to make a pillow under his head
in the tight cave of creation.
Come spring, God will wake,
yawn, in a surge of smiling
realization gather all to him,
bring us out into a kind of noon—
a commodiousness, incandescence
we can't imagine. Of course
tiny creatures like us won't
notice much difference.
It's for the greater creatures—
the far away titans, the planet
walkers whose hearts
hourly lubdub oceans—
to linger, muse, fret about
whether spring will ever come.

Cohort

Right now, five thousand species
of bacteria swirl in your viscera,
and every individual of every one,
a space traveler. Think of how vast
you are: the trip some make at speeds
unimaginable down your gullet
into the galactic core of your gut,
and those who venture farther—
twenty-five feet of intestine,
a wormhole from universe
to universe, the second
distinct, dry, bright, again
unimaginable. So I ponder also
the creature we must inhabit, you
and I, two species among millions—
I ponder it in its "daily" (is it
bound by time?) operations, wonder
about the losses it knows, petty
hurts and exultations though
on a scale far grander than we
can imagine. And the anti-
biotics of a big bang: how do, how
can the little traumas of this ship
register—as I ply intestine, gawk
at the vast formations
of cilia and sphincter as if
Biblical miracles, as I careen
from thinking this creature
worthless to thinking it God—
God like I must be to the universe
inside me, to those consciousnesses
I can't imagine, but who must
spend their lonely hours in
silent contemplation of mine.

Starlight

When I see starlight, I marvel
the thousands of years it traveled
to meet me, before I was even
conceived, and think myself
a sort of time vector—a very
short one—in the midst of lines
that stretch along farther than I
can imagine. Behind me are things
evolving which that star's light
is on its way toward, and each will
know itself the final destination—
though the light threads itself
through them like a needlepoint:
stitches them and me together
in contemplation of an image
of the past. Tell me, human,
what does that make you think
of time? That light from a star
no longer existent on its way
to a creature not yet evolved
can thread you up; that you, pearl,
string along with creatures altogether
like and unlike you? If you were
a space traveler, it would sing
to you of comfort. If you were
a space traveler, you'd call it love.

His Heaven

Is not so very different from the ship,
is in fact the ship exactly—
screen of stars, hamster-trail halls
to scurry from room to room,
and the ever-hovering promise
of change: space unfolding
infinitely, unending time
experienced as unending space
apprehended as unending
possibility. Another traveler?
Would he, by foreclosing possibility,
foreclose the possibility of Heaven?
Evenings, drunk on silence,
the space traveler can't imagine
how another could be anything
but crack and jangle. If Heaven
is a sound, it is the bare resistance
of space as the ship glides past,
but if it is a texture, it is the feel
of another hand, mitts off.
If it is a sight, it must be the colors
of stars, but if a smell, then the damp
earthiness that everywhere
in the universe signifies breath.
Asking a space traveler to imagine
a Heaven he could enjoy—
isn't that like asking God
to fashion a stone he can't lift?

His Birthday

Because our planet's so far from its star,
birthdays come rarely and my species
finds other ways to mark our passage—
most associated with the body's various
sproutings, the blemishes and growths
that indicate time getting on. For my
First Forehead Crease, I was given
a rocket-ship model kit and promptly told
not to look so concerned about how many
pieces it contained. Soon I set up a table
in the basement—an unhinged door
laid horizontal on two sawhorses—
and started to pluck pieces one by one
from their plastic trees. By the time I was
ready to paint it silver, other passages
had come and gone: Pitch Deepenings,
Wax Cleanings, Assorted Bone Nubs
and Their Removal from My Face. It was
a wholly different me, nearly, hunching
in that basement, applying a silver patina
to a model of what even then looked like
my future. I spray-painted in a gentle
back-and-forth motion, from a foot away
created a chrome cloud, and saw
as I advanced up the body how the model
in that faded space turned to glistening.
Just like now, I think, landed, polishing
the three fins on which this ship sits,
running a rag over its arched doorway,
balancing a rickety ladder against
its curved chrome skin and waxing
the nose cone till it shines like an obelisk.
And celebrating, too, if more quietly,
rites of diminishment: Hurt Back Day,

Unwanted Hair Day (stretched to a week
since so many sites are involved), and
Name Forgetting Day, slightly delayed
in companionless space. Party hat on,
mulling in my Captain's Chair—new stars,
new starts rushing toward me, Stained
Teeth Day, too, quickly approaching—
I become pensive, like a human standing
with arms out, palms up, making his body
a scale for opposing points of view—
on the one hand, a rustless realization;
on the other, corporeal dust.

His Aubade

The ship's tic: the ship ticks. I heat
water, drape a blanket on my shoulders, turn
row after row of dials and pause to watch
light meet light—blue lineaments of keyboard
and screen defining themselves against
brushed nickel. Then I click on day:
churn of heat, glow along the floor
rising from pink flush to the blue-lipped
white of the star under which I was born.
It is never dawn out here, or always,
so I sleep from exhaustion to hunger,
am content to lose track of lapsing time.
When you think of space, remember
that it's filled with such ships, that we
cross and cross in unmarried vastness—
the sheer, continental cliff of a galaxy's edge,
and beyond, an immense gulf of darkness
before that bright grain, a tiny star
punctuating night, announcing the cliff edge
of a new galaxy—a gulf that has no equal
except the caverns of perception. Maybe.
Half the ships out here ferry space travelers
dead since old stars started, or so lost
in inner expanse that they simply drift,
bright thumbnail clipping slowly
running down into darkness, like a clock
whose second hand circles slower
and slower in a silent, unlit house.

Notes

"The Great Moon Hoax, 1835" refers to a series of articles detailing the discovery of life on the Moon published in *The Sun*, a New York newspaper, beginning on August 25, 1835.

"His Father's Missing Brother" is for Freddy Grossberg, who disappeared from Brooklyn in the late 1970s.

"The Great Filter" refers to a theory connected with the Fermi Paradox, the apparent contradiction between the likelihood of extraterrestrial civilizations and our inability (so far) to find evidence of them. The theory proposes that some filter might exist, some inhibition to civilizations advancing beyond a certain point.

"Earth" uses a low-end estimate of how much junk is currently orbiting our planet, and, of course, we add more all the time.

"The Oil Spill" refers to the aftermath of the explosion aboard the *Deepwater Horizon* drilling rig, which occurred on April 20, 2010 in the Gulf of Mexico.

Roy G. Biv in "He Pities Humans" is a mnemonic for recalling the order of the spectrum of visible light.

"Boston" and "He Addresses the Native, Sometime Later" are for Peter Bunnell. "His Crush" is for Stephen MarcAurele. "He Warns Another Traveler" is for Dave Seguin. "His Pirate" is for Michael Bartha. "Wisdom" is for Sean Michael Morris. Many of the other poems are for Steven R. Young.

Acknowledgments

Grateful acknowledgment is made to the journals in which these poems appeared, here listed with their original titles:

American Literary Review: "The Space Traveler and Home"

Barrow Street: "The Space Traveler and Notes" and "The Space Traveler and Black Holes"

Bat City Review: "The Space Traveler and Life Expectancy"

Bellingham Review: "The Space Traveler and Depilation" and "The Space Traveler's Heaven"

Cave Wall: "The Space Traveler and Google Universe," "The Space Traveler's Heaven," and "The Space Traveler Talks Frankly about Desire"

Cincinnati Review: "The Space Traveler's Aubade"

Connecticut Review: "The Space Traveler's Oil Spill" and "The Space Traveler and Meaning"

Cream City Review: "The Space Traveler's Funk" and "The Space Traveler and the Planetary Observer"

Drunken Boat: "The Space Traveler's Birthday" and "The Space Traveler's Duende"

The Gay & Lesbian Review: "The Space Traveler and Star-light"

Green Mountains Review: "The Space Traveler and Wandering," "The Space Traveler's Pirate," and "The Space Traveler and Earth"

Greensboro Review: "The Space Traveler's Warning"

Gulf Coast: "The Space Traveler's Tense"

Hotel Amerika: "The Space Traveler's Brother" and "The Space Traveler Pities Us"

Hunger Mountain (print and online editions): "Space Traveler, Time, Alone," "The Space Traveler and God," and "The Space Traveler Awaits a Call"

Indiana Review: "The Space Traveler's Contented Moments"

The Journal: "The Space Traveler and Home" and "The Space Travelers' Book of Wisdom"

Kestral: "The Space Traveler and Black Holes" and "The Space Traveler's View Screen"

Literary Imagination: "The Space Traveler and the Promised Planet"

Malahat Review: "The Space Traveler's Dream" and "Space Traveler, Time Travel"

Mid-American Review: "The Space Traveler and the Promised Planet" and "The Space Traveler's Hope"

Missouri Review: "The Space Traveler's Husband," "The Space Traveler and Wandering," "Space Traveler, Great Filter," "The Space Traveler and Crop Circles," "The Space Traveler's Husband," and "The Space Traveler and Runaway Stars"

National Poetry Review: "The Space Traveler's Shame"

Natural Bridge: "The Space Traveler's Nightmare"

New England Review: "Why the Space Traveler Declines"

Notre Dame Review: "The Space Traveler and the Great Moon Hoax, 1835," "The Space Traveler and Orbital Decay," and "Space Traveler Sex"

North American Review: "The Space Traveler's Aisling"

Ninth Letter: "The Space Traveler and the Doppler Effect"

Rattle: "The Space Traveler's Moon" and "The Space Traveler's Crush"

Superstition Review: "The Space Traveler's Father's Missing Brother" and "The Space Traveler's Heaven"

Tampa Review: "The Space Traveler's Missives," "The Space Traveler Falls in Love," "The Space Traveler Pities Us," and "The Space Traveler's Calculus"

Washington Square: "The Space Traveler and Boston"

Whiskey Island: "The Space Traveler and Earth"

Zone 3: "The Space Traveler's Visitor" and "The Space Traveler and Restless Leg Syndrome"

"The Space Traveler Talks Frankly about Desire" also appeared in *The Best American Poetry 2011*, Kevin Young, ed. (Scribner, 2011) and *Flicker and Spark: A Contemporary Queer Anthology of Spoken Word and Poetry*, Regie Cabio and Brittany Fonte, eds. (Lowbrow, 2013).

"The Space Traveler's Tense" was republished on *Verse Daily* (November 7, 2011).

"The Space Traveler's Husband" and "Why the Space Traveler Declines" were republished on the Lambda Literary Foundation website, October 2010 (www.lambdaliterary.org).

"The Space Traveler and Wandering" was distributed as a broadside by *Broadsided*, July 2009 (www.broadsidedpress.org).

"The Space Traveler on Meryl Streep" appeared in *Divining Divas: 100 Gay Men on Their Muses*, Michael Montlack, ed. (Lethe, 2011).

Thanks also to the Connecticut Commission on Culture and Tourism, the Faculty Senate of the University of Hartford, and to Dean Joseph Voelker of the College of Arts & Sciences at the University of Hartford for grants which enabled the completion of this book.

I am especially grateful to those who gave friendship and support: Steven R. Young, Maggie Anderson, Peter Bunnell, Marc Civitarese, Mark Doty, Cody Enloe, James Finnegan, Gray Jacobik, Leslie McGrath, Clare Rossini, Paul Simmons, Bryan Sinche, and Sarah Pemberton Strong.

And, finally, my thanks to Cassandra Mendoza, the artists Samuel Ringler and Autumn Von Plinsky, Sean Donnelly, and, for his kindness, patience, and dedication to bookmaking as an art, Richard Mathews.

This book is in memory of T.—

I loved thee, Spirit, and love, nor can
The soul of Shakespeare love thee more.

About the Author

Originally from Far Rockaway, New York, Benjamin S. Grossberg was educated at Rutgers and the University of Houston. From 2000 to 2008, he worked at Antioch College in Ohio, where he purchased a small farm and planted the Granny Smith orchard for which his second book was named. He is currently Director of Creative Writing and an Associate Professor of English at the University of Hartford, in Hartford, Connecticut.

Ben is the author of two previous books of poetry, *Sweet Core Orchard* (University of Tampa, 2009), winner of the Tampa Review Prize for Poetry and a Lambda Literary Award, and *Underwater Lengths in a Single Breath* (Ashland Poetry Press, 2007), winner of the Snyder Prize. He also published a chapbook, *The Auctioneer Bangs his Gavel*, with Kent State University Press (2006). His poems have appeared widely, including in the Pushcart Prize and Best American Poetry anthologies, *Poetry Daily* and *Verse Daily*, and the magazines *Paris Review, Southwest Review, New England Review, Missouri Review*, and *The Sun*. A recipient of individual artist grants from the states of Ohio and Connecticut, he serves as Assistant Poetry Editor and regular book reviewer for the *Antioch Review*.

Ben is also a distance runner and a vegetarian, and lives with a small, unnamed cat.

About the Book

Space Traveler is set in Aldus and Optima types, designed by Hermann Zapf. They were both originally designed for casting as metal types at the Stempel foundry in Germany. Aldus (1954) hearkens back to the Venetian types used by Aldus Manutius in the fifteenth century; Optima (1958) is a sans serif with a more contemporary look, but with modified strokes that show the influence of calligraphy. The cover painting is original work done in acrylic by Autumn Von Plinsky, a free-lance illustrator based in New Haven, Connecticut. Her work can be found on the web at www. autumnvonplinsky.com. The engravings here reproduced as section dividers were done on aluminum and copper plates by Samuel Ringler, a freelance artist based in Northridge, California. The book was designed and typeset by Richard Mathews, in consultation with the author, at the University of Tampa Press. It has been printed on acid-free recycled text paper in support of the Green Press Initiative.

POETRY FROM THE UNIVERSITY OF TAMPA PRESS

John R. Bensko, *Visitations*◊

John Blair, *The Occasions of Paradise**

Jenny Browne, *At Once*

Jenny Browne, *The Second Reason*

Jenny Browne, *Dear Stranger*

Christopher Buckley, *Rolling the Bones**

Christopher Buckley, *White Shirt*

Richard Chess, *Chair in the Desert*

Richard Chess, *Tekiah*

Richard Chess, *Third Temple*

Kevin Jeffery Clarke, *The Movie of Us*

Jane Ellen Glasser, *Light Persists**

Benjamin S. Grossberg, *Sweet Core Orchard**

Benjamin S. Grossberg, *Space Traveler*

Michael Hettich, *Systems of Vanishing**

Dennis Hinrichsen, *Rip-tooth**

Kathleen Jesme, *Fire Eater*

Jennifer Key, *The Old Dominion**

Steve Kowit, *The First Noble Truth**

Lance Larsen, *Backyard Alchemy*

Lance Larsen, *Genius Loci*

Lance Larsen, *In All Their Animal Brilliance**

Julia B. Levine, *Ask**

Julia B. Levine, *Ditch-tender*

Sarah Maclay, *Whore**

Sarah Maclay, *The White Bride*

Sarah Maclay, *Music for the Black Room*

Peter Meinke, *Lines from Neuchâtel*

John Willis Menard, *Lays in Summer Lands*

Kent Shaw, *Calenture**

Barry Silesky, *This Disease*

Jordan Smith, *For Appearances**

Jordan Smith, *The Names of Things Are Leaving*

Jordan Smith, *The Light in the Film*

Lisa M. Steinman, *Carslaw's Sequences*

Lisa M. Steinman, *Absence & Presence*

Marjorie Stelmach, *Bent upon Light*

Marjorie Stelmach, *A History of Disappearance*

Ira Sukrungruang, *In Thailand It Is Night*◊

Richard Terrill, *Coming Late to Rachmaninoff*

Richard Terrill, *Almost Dark*

Matt Yurdana, *Public Gestures*

* Denotes winner of the Tampa Review Prize for Poetry
◊ Denotes winner of the Anita Claire Scharf Award